CONTEMPORARY BIOGRAPHIES

DUA LIPA

by Heather L. Bode

BrightPoint Press
San Diego, CA

BrightPoint Press

an imprint of ReferencePoint Press, Inc.
Printed in the United States

For more information, contact:
BrightPoint Press
PO Box 27779
San Diego, CA 92198
www.BrightPointPress.com

LIBRARY OF CONGRESS CATALOGING-IN-PUBLICATION DATA

Names: Bode, Heather L. author
Title: Dua Lipa / by Heather L. Bode.
Description: San Diego, CA: ReferencePoint Press, 2026. | Series: Contemporary biographies | Includes bibliographical references and index. | Audience: Grades 7–9
Identifiers: LCCN 2025018130 (print) | LCCN 2025018131 (eBook) | ISBN 9781678211523 hardcover | ISBN 9781678211530 eBook
Subjects: LCSH: Lipa, Dua, 1995---Juvenile literature | Singers--Biography--Juvenile literature | LCGFT: Biographies
Classification: LCC ML3930.L563 B63 2025 (print) | LCC ML3930.L563 (eBook) | DDC 782.42164092 [B]--dc23/eng/20250411
LC record available at https://lccn.loc.gov/2025018130
LC eBook record available at https://lccn.loc.gov/2025018131

CONTENTS

AT A GLANCE

- Dua Lipa was born in London, United Kingdom, on August 22, 1995. She has one sister and one brother.

- Dua had dreamed of being a pop star since she was little. She took classes at London's Sylvia Young Theatre School on weekends.

- When Dua was 11, her family returned to Kosovo. Her parents had fled Kosovo to escape war before Dua was born. Dua was influenced by hip-hop, which was popular there.

- At 15, Dua moved back to London. She knew she needed to be there to pursue her dream.

- Dua filmed a commercial for a TV reality singing competition called *The X-Factor*. This helped her get managers.

- Dua signed with Warner Brothers Records in 2014. Her first album, *Dua Lipa*, came out in 2017.
- Dua has won many music awards, including three Grammys and seven BRIT Awards. She is one of the top female recording artists in the world.
- Dua stays busy outside of music. She models, acts, and is a voice for underrepresented groups.

A LIFE-CHANGING MOMENT

Dua Lipa's life changed in 3 minutes and 29 seconds. That is the length of her song "New Rules." When it was released on July 7, 2017, Lipa was about 2 months away from turning 22. She did not write the song. But she could relate to it personally. Listeners around the world felt the same way.

"New Rules" is a breakup song. In the song, the singer's relationship is over.

Dua Lipa started playing live shows in 2016, including a stop in Austin, Texas, for the South by Southwest music festival.

She loves him, but he does not love her. In the song, Lipa sings about three new rules. First, do not pick up the phone. Second, do not let him back into your life. Third, do not be his friend. These rules help the singer move on with her life. "New Rules" was produced using electronic dance music. This gives the song a dance-club feel.

The music video for "New Rules" was released at the same time. More details in the video made it appealing, especially to women. The music video was set in a hotel named The Confidante. A confidante is someone a person can trust with secrets. At first, Lipa appears to be alone in a hotel. Then the camera angle widens. She is surrounded by friends. Her friends help Lipa follow the three rules. They are there to

Lipa had the support of dancers when she performed at the UEFA Champions League soccer final in Kyiv, Ukraine, in May 2018.

support her. By the end of the video, Lipa helps another friend. She is going through a similar breakup. Flamingoes appear at the end of the video. Lipa wanted to include them because they travel in flocks. They are united, just as she is with her friends.

"New Rules" became Lipa's first major hit in the United States. Before its release,

Lipa attended the American Music Awards in Los Angeles in 2018.

she was opening for other artists such as Bruno Mars. After the song's success, she was headlining her own shows in America. She was on a global stage.

A RISING STAR

"New Rules" was just one of many hit songs for Dua Lipa. This single song has been streamed more than 1 billion times on Spotify. Since the release of "New Rules," Lipa has had 23 songs make the Billboard Hot 100 list through 2024. Five of those songs have made the top ten. She's also won several awards. This includes three Grammys and seven BRIT Awards. Over her career, Lipa has accumulated a net worth of $35 million. How she did it defies the odds.

FAMILY BEFORE FAME

Dua Lipa was born into an Albanian family. Albania is a small country east of Italy. It borders Greece and Kosovo. *Dua* means "love" in Albanian.

Before Dua was born, her parents lived in Kosovo. Most people living in Kosovo are Albanian. Albanians are an **ethnic group**. Until the early 1990s, Kosovo was part of Yugoslavia. Yugoslavia was a **communist** country. It had many ethnic groups. It also

From age 11 to 15, Dua lived in Pristina, Kosovo, with her family.

Gotë me
fruta!

had many religions, including Islam and Christianity. When communism fell, new political leaders wanted to gain control. They created mistrust among ethnic groups. Civil war broke out. For their safety, the Lipas moved to the United Kingdom in 1992. Dua was born in London, United Kingdom, on August 22, 1995.

MUSIC DREAMS

Dua grew up in a musical family. Her father had been a singer in a band called Oda.

Dua's Siblings

Dua Lipa is the oldest of three children. Her younger sister, Rina, has many talents. She is a model and an actress. She is also a singer. Lipa's youngest sibling is her brother, Gjin. He works in the music industry, too. Gjin is a music producer.

She would watch him from backstage. Dua listened to live music with her family when they were on vacation. They stayed out late. But Dua thought it was fun. Dua wanted to be a musician.

Like her father, Dua loved to sing. Dua went to Fitzjohn's Primary School in London. Her music teacher once asked if anyone wanted to try out for the school choir. Dua volunteered. She stood up in front of the whole school. The music teacher played the piano. Dua tried to sing. But she could not hit the high note. Everyone laughed.

But that didn't stop her. She took singing lessons on weekends at Sylvia Young Theatre School. There, she found a new music teacher who saw her talent. "When I

While attending Fitzjohn's Primary School, Dua took cello lessons.

started at Sylvia Young, my teacher there told me, 'You *can* sing, and don't let anyone tell you what you can and can't do,'" Dua said. "That really helped me. It opened my eyes. I was really young and didn't have to listen to anyone else if I believed in myself."[1] With this new confidence and the support of her new teacher, Dua sang in front of her class again. She was 9. This time, she sang in a lower **register**. Her voice had deeper tones. Dua moved up to a class with 14- and 15-year-olds.

When Dua was 11, her family moved back to Kosovo. It was safe for them to return, and her father got a job. While there, she listened to a lot of music. She says,

> *People in Kosovo listen to a lot of hip-hop music. So when I lived there, it was . . . a lot of Biggie and Tupac and 50 Cent and Snoop Dogg . . . and Method Man and Redman, [which] was my first show. All my dreams about music and performing involve being on stage. But I think it was just a dream . . . [I was] trying to figure out how you get to that point.*[2]

A TEENAGER IN LONDON

Dua wanted to return to London. This is where she could pursue her pop-star dreams. At 14, she talked to her parents about going back. She told them being in London would help her finish high school. Then she could get into a university. Her parents eventually agreed. Dua returned to London when she was 15. Her father said, "She was always very mature, even at 15."[3]

Dua went to school. She also started posting music videos on social media. She sang **cover songs** of singers such as Alicia Keys and Christina Aguilera.

School became less important to Dua as she followed her dreams. She often skipped class. Eventually, she was expelled. Her parents told her she had two options.

While in London, Dua lived with an older friend of her family in Camden, a borough of the city.

She could find a different school to complete her education. Or she could return to Kosovo. Dua wanted to stay in London. Dua attended Parliament Hill School. This was a school for girls. Dua completed high school. But she did not go to college.

Dua worked three jobs. She was a hostess at a Mexican restaurant called La Bodega Negra. She was also a door supervisor at a nightclub. And Dua worked for a modeling agency. She thought this might help her meet people in the music business. When she was 17, Dua filmed a commercial for *The X Factor*. This is a reality TV singing competition. Dua played

Lipa worked as a hostess at La Bodega Negra in London, where she once showed Channing Tatum and his wife to their table.

a contestant with dreams of being the next winner. She sang a cover of the song "Lost in Music." Dua never entered the competition. But the commercial's producer offered her a deal to publish her music. She took it to a lawyer for advice. The lawyer said she needed a manager.

STEPPING INTO ADULTHOOD

In 2013, Lipa turned 18. She signed with TaP Music Publishing. Her managers were Ben Mawson and Ed Millet. They gave her access to music studios. Lipa worked at La Bodega Negra in the evenings. Afterward, she went to nightclubs to dance. This is where she got her inspiration for creating her own music. She slept for a few hours before going to work in the music studio.

Eventually, this schedule became too much. Lipa quit her restaurant job. TaP Music paid her a monthly income instead. This way, she could focus on writing.

Becoming a pop star was not easy. Lipa worked fiercely throughout her teenage years. Her dad had always told her that she needed to work hard. But one needs a little luck, too. *The X Factor* commercial was the bit of luck Lipa needed. It had led to signing with managers. They could introduce her to record labels.

Lipa takes the stage at a festival in the Netherlands in 2018.

CHAPTER TWO

SUCCESSES AND CHALLENGES

Lipa already had a distinct, husky voice. But she was singing cover songs. She needed her own music. Lipa had her first professional writing session right after signing with TaP Music.

Lipa knew she wanted to sing pop music. It made her want to dance. But she was influenced by hip-hop. She liked rapper J. Cole and singers such as P!NK and Nelly Furtado. One song from her early writing

As an up-and-coming pop star, Lipa posted performances on YouTube and SoundCloud. Eventually she went on tour, playing a number of shows at music festivals around the world.

sessions was "Hotter than Hell." This song set the sound of her first album. Lipa called it dark pop. To her, that meant uplifting melodies with lyrics where the artist reflects on her life.

By the middle of 2014, Lipa's managers had spread the word about their rising star. Warner Brothers Music needed a female pop star for their label. After meeting with Lipa, they offered her a deal. Lipa's parents flew to London when she signed the contract.

BECOMING A POP STAR

Signing with a major record label was a big step toward Lipa's dream. But she did not realize how much work it took to be a pop star. She needed to learn how to perform

The Lipa family met with Warner Brothers Music executives in London to review and sign the recording contract.

for live audiences. She had to work on her stage presence. She did not know how to promote a record. And she didn't know how to handle social media backlash. In addition, pop stars often go on tour.

This means spending time away from friends and family.

Lipa also needed to continue to develop her songwriting. This was important to her. It was also important to Warner Brothers. Being a songwriter set Lipa apart from other rising stars. Lipa worked with

Dua Lipa writes her songs in a notebook she bought from a CVS pharmacy.

professional songwriters. They showed her how to write. But it felt odd telling them her deepest thoughts. So Lipa started asking them questions about their own lives. Having these conversations helped her. She became open and honest about what she wanted to say in her songs.

One of her favorite songwriters to work with was Stephen Kozmeniuk. "Koz" had worked with Madonna and Nicki Minaj. He became a trusted friend and cowriter.

DUA LIPA

Lipa's self-titled first album was released in June 2017. Lipa co-wrote most of the album. She sang about her own life. But she also focused on events in her friends' lives. She wrote about what happened at the dance clubs. She even wrote about working at La Bodega Negra.

Lipa performed her global hit "New Rules" at the BRIT Awards 2018. Afterward, she faced backlash on social media. One person criticized her lack of energy and her dance skills. This stuck with Lipa. She was made into a meme. Some people felt she did not deserve the awards she was winning. Lipa was hurt and humiliated.

But she did not give up. "All that was happening while I was 22, 23 years old and still growing up. You have to build tough skin. You have to be resilient," she said.[4] Lipa worked hard to prove her critics wrong. She promoted her album on tour and focused on new music. In November 2019, her critics changed their minds. At the

Lipa wore an elaborate gown designed by Giambattista Valli to the 2018 BRIT Awards.

At the 2019 BRIT Awards, Lipa won the award for best single for "One Kiss," a duet with singer and songwriter Calvin Harris.

MTV Europe Music Awards, Lipa performed "Don't Start Now" from her upcoming second album. Her energy and dance moves captivated the audience.

FUTURE NOSTALGIA

Lipa's second album was released in March 2020. It was called *Future Nostalgia*. Nostalgia means a longing for the past. This album had a retro disco feel. Yet, it seemed fresh. It was meant for live performance. Lipa's songs were less about her personal life. They focused on universal emotions such as love.

But just as the album came out, the world shut down. The COVID-19 pandemic was raging. Countries around the world enforced lockdowns. Concerts and other events were cancelled. Many people were stuck at home.

Future Nostalgia was an upbeat album. It was filled with fresh dance tunes. Lipa wanted her songs to be played in clubs. The pandemic prevented that. But the songs still appealed to listeners. She sang from her apartment on *The Late Late Show with James Cordon*. People still

The Challenges of Songwriting

Songwriters often pen many, many songs for a single album. Choosing which ones to use can be a challenge. Lipa worked on 160 songs for her first album. Only twelve made it on the album. For *Future Nostalgia*, eleven songs were chosen out of about 150. Lipa is dedicated to songwriting. Her confidence has grown with her years of experience.

danced to her songs. But they danced in their living rooms instead of in a club.

Lipa's song "Levitating" was the top song on the Billboard Year-End Hot 100 singles of 2021. Lipa's album came at a time when people did not have much optimism. Her upbeat songs gave them this gift. Other artists released albums at that time. But it was Lipa's album that won her the title of Quarantine Queen.

RADICAL OPTIMISM

Lipa's third album, *Radical Optimism*, came out in May 2024. She opened the 2024 Grammy Awards with performances of her songs "Houdini" and "Training Season." Her goal for the third album was to make people happy.

Lipa returned to writing about personal experiences. "Houdini" has a message. It is about knowing your worth. This makes it easier to decide when it's time to leave bad situations. Lipa did not understand this when she was younger. But now she did. She said,

> *I've also made peace with the fact that people are going to make up scenarios about me. . . . I've also allowed myself to be ok with so many of those things because I get to do what I love every single day.*[5]

During her *Radical Optimism* tour, Lipa performed in fifty-five cities around the world.

CHAPTER THREE

HARD WORK PAYS OFF

When she was younger, Lipa had big dreams. She imagined singing at a certain festival and on a certain stage. In June 2024, that dream came true. Lipa headlined the Glastonbury Festival. It is the world's largest music festival. She even sang on the Pyramid Stage. This was the exact stage she imagined in her dreams.

About 100,000 people came to see her. They sang along to "Be the One," a song

Dua Lipa has performed at the Glastonbury Festival twice, once in 2017 and again in 2024.

After performing at the Glastonbury Festival's Pyramid Stage in 2024, Lipa danced with fans and friends on the festival grounds until 6:00 in the morning.

from her first album. It had been 9 years since the song was released. Back then, it was not an instant hit. She told the crowd that they were making her dreams come true.

AWARDS

Lipa was being recognized by the music industry as well. Between 2017 and 2024, She was nominated for ten Grammys and won three. These included Best Dance Recording and Best New Artist in 2019. She also won Best Pop Vocal Album for *Future Nostalgia*.

The BRIT Awards honor British artists. In 2018, Lipa won British Breakthrough Act and British Female Solo Artist. In 2024, she won Best Pop Act. This was her seventh win at the BRIT Awards.

In 2020, iHeart Radio awarded Lipa two Titanium Awards. These are special awards given when a song hits 1 billion **audience spins** on iHeartRadio stations. They were for the songs "Break My Heart" and "Don't

Start Now." She won the award again in 2021 for "Levitating." All three songs were from her album, *Future Nostalgia*. MTV sponsors yearly Video Music Awards, or VMAs. In 2024, her "Houdini" video won Best Choreography.

COLLABORATIONS

Radio stations often play songs that feature collaborations. This is when another musician sings on a song, or track, of

World Records

According to Guinness World Records, Lipa holds two world records. In 2020, she broke the record for most tickets sold for a live streamed concert by a solo female artist. In 2021, she broke the record for most monthly listeners on Spotify for a female artist in a 1-year period.

an album. Collaborating can expand a singer's fan base. It also increases the chances that a song will be a hit.

Lipa has collaborated with many famous musicians. R&B artist Miguel and Coldplay's Chris Martin were featured on her first album. She worked with Calvin Harris on "One Kiss." Italian opera singer Andrea Bocelli invited her to sing on his 2018 album.

Future Nostalgia featured guests such as Pharrell Williams, Nile Rodgers, and Diplo. A remix album called *Club Future Nostalgia* featured Madonna, Missy Elliott, and K-Pop stars BLACKPINK.

In 2022, Lipa collaborated with music legend Elton John. Their song "Cold Heart" introduced Lipa to older generations.

Lipa paused for a photo with Elton John at a 2021 event put on by his foundation.

It became a number-one hit on charts around the world. On his final concert tour of North America, John talked about Lipa:

> *I adore her. She is incredibly talented—absolutely brilliant—and so professional. It's a pleasure to be around someone who is so young, has done so much already and is so humble. She is also great fun, and we got on like a house on fire.*[6]

BY THE NUMBERS

In March 2024, Lipa became the first female artist to have four songs with more than 2 billion streams on Spotify. The songs were "Don't Start Now," "One Kiss," "New Rules," and "Levitating." Other popular artists such as Billie Eilish and Olivia Rodrigo came close to having this many streams. But Lipa stood alone with this honor.

By the end of 2024, Lipa's fans had streamed her music more than 45 billion times. She became one of the top female recording artists in the world. *Time* magazine named her one of their 100 most influential people in 2024. This award shows that there is more to Lipa. She is not limited to writing and singing music. She has goals outside of the music industry.

DUA LIPA'S CAREER TIMELINE

♫ **2004**
Dua takes classes at Sylvia Young Theatre School.

♫ **2012**
Dua signs with TaP Music.

♫ **2014**
Lipa signs with Warner Brothers Music.

♫ **2017**
Lipa's first album, *Dua Lipa*, is released.

♫ **2018**
Lipa wins two BRIT Awards.

♫ **2019**
Lipa wins two Grammys.

♫ **2020**
Lipa's second album, *Future Nostalgia*, is released.

♫ **2021**
Lipa wins her third Grammy.

♫ **2024**
Lipa's third album, *Radical Optimism*, is released.

Source: "Dua Lipa," Encyclopaedia Britannica*, March 24, 2025, www.britannica.*

In a little over a decade, Dua Lipa built an award-winning career as a pop musician. This timeline details her major accomplishments along the way.

CHAPTER FOUR

LIFE BEYOND MUSIC

Some pop stars might be content to write and record music. But Lipa has shown a relentless level of energy. She seems driven to do more. Whether collaborating with others or working on her own, Dua keeps busy in many ways.

Lipa has revisited some jobs she did early on in her career. These include modeling and acting. Lipa is also passionate about expressing her thoughts and beliefs.

Lipa (second from right) has a close bond with her family, including her father Dukagjin (left), mother Anesa (second from left), sister Rina (right), and brother Gjin (not pictured).

She does this through songs. But she also acts on those beliefs through advocacy programs and by posting online.

MODELING AND FASHION DESIGN

Fashion has always been important to Lipa. She started a fashion blog called *Dua Daily* when she was 17. This gave her experience with followers and influencers. Lipa pursued modeling as a teenager. She has been a brand ambassador for Puma, Evian, and Yves Saint Laurent. Brand ambassadors are featured in a company's advertisements.

In 2023, Lipa announced a clothing collection for Versace. She did not have formal design training. But she liked sketching designs. Lipa had done some modeling work for Versace. She texted a

Lipa wore a sleek, custom-designed Versace gown with Versace pumps to the Versace FW23 Show at the Pacific Design Center in March 2023.

sketch to Donatella Versace. The famous designer thought Lipa showed some talent. She gave Lipa a chance.

ACTING

Lipa is also interested in acting. In 2023, she made a **cameo** appearance as a mermaid in the movie *Barbie.* This film featured her song "Dance the Night." Lipa also starred in *Argylle*, a 2024 spy action film. She played the character LaGrange.

Lipa has acted in commercials as well. In 2023, she signed a contract with Porsche. The car company needed a commercial for its new electric car. Lipa cowrote, codirected, and starred in the commercial.

ACTIVISM

Lipa understands her fame gives her opportunities to speak up. She has a worldwide audience. She often uses her voice for **activism**.

In January 2024, Lipa appeared at the premiere of *Argylle*, which was held at Odeon Luxe Leicester Square in London, England.

Lipa has always been close to her family. Being the child of **immigrants** shaped her values and her work ethic. She said, "You understand something on a personal level: That no **refugee** leaves their country without having to."[7]

To help her parents' homeland, Lipa and her father started the Sunny Hill Foundation. This foundation works to support Kosovo's most vulnerable populations. It also works to fund the arts. The foundation has supported many school music programs.

In addition, Sunny Hill Foundation hosts The Sunny Hill Festival. This is a multiday music event. It brings musicians from around the world to Pristina, Kosovo. The festival also draws tourists to Kosovo. They spend a lot of money, which helps support area businesses.

In 2024, Lipa became The Trevor Project's Mental Health Champion of the Year. This award goes to someone

Lipa and her father performed in front of more than 20,000 fans during her first show in Pristina, Kosovo, in 2016.

who advocates for mental health issues in LGBTQ+ youth. She said,

> *I am unbelievably moved and honored to receive this year's Mental Health Champion of the Year Award. The Trevor Project is an organization that is near and dear to my heart, and I am humbled to play a part in shining*

Lipa, who has been open about her own mental health issues, has supported The Trevor Project's mission of advocating for the mental health of the LGBTQ+ community.

a light on mental health awareness for LGBTQ+ young people.[8]

From a little girl auditioning for the school choir to a legendary pop star, Dua Lipa always showed spunk and determination. She called it an immigrant work ethic. Through her teenage years, she adapted with each success and challenge.

"I have this outlook on rolling with the punches, if things are bad, they're never going to be bad for too long . . . you're just going to navigate and move through it." Lipa has grown into a confident and resilient woman. And she takes nothing for granted. She says, "I feel so lucky that this is my life and I get to do this."[9]

Service95

Service95 is Lipa's website. It provides a place for people to read articles about rights for women, refugees, and the LGBTQ+ community. From Service95, Lipa's podcast, *At Your Service*, can be accessed. She interviews musicians, authors, and filmmakers. The site gives Lipa's fans a backstage pass into her thoughts.

GLOSSARY

activism

working for social change

audience spins

the number of times a song plays on the radio

cameo

a brief appearance in a movie or TV show by a famous person

communist

a form of government that controls the economy and owns all the property

cover songs

songs performed by someone other than the original artist

ethnic group

people who share a common culture, religion, ancestry, or traditions

immigrants

people who move to different countries to live permanently

refugee

someone forced to leave a country due to war or persecution

register

the range of notes a person can sing

SOURCE NOTES

CHAPTER ONE: FAMILY BEFORE FAME

1. Quoted in "The Wylde Interview: Dua Lipa," *Wylde Magazine*, April 5, 2019. https://wyldemag.com.

2. Quoted in "Dua Lipa on Leaving Bad Relationships and Choosing Radical Optimism." *YouTube*, uploaded by Q with Tom Power. May 3, 2024. www.youtube.com.

3. Quoted in Anderson Cooper, "Dua Lipa: The 60 Minutes Interview." *YouTube*, uploaded by 60 Minutes. September 16, 2024. www.youtube.com.

CHAPTER TWO: SUCCESSES AND CHALLENGES

4. Quoted in Jazmin Tolliver, "Dua Lipa Reflects on Becoming a 'Humiliating' Meme After Awards Show Fail." *HuffPost*, May 5, 2024. www.huffpost.com.

5. Quoted in "Dua Lipa on Leaving Bad Relationships."

CHAPTER THREE: HARD WORK PAYS OFF

6. Quoted in Jem Aswad, "How Elton John and Dua Lipa's 'Cold Heart' Pulsed to Life—and Became a Surprise Global Hit." *Variety*, November 30, 2022. https//variety.com.

CHAPTER FOUR: LIFE BEYOND MUSIC

7. Quoted in Caroline Sullivan, *Dua Lipa: The Unauthorized Biography*. Michael O'Mara Books, 2023, p. 24.

8. Quoted in Stephen Daw, "Dua Lipa Heralded as the Trevor Project's Mental Health Champion of the Year." *Billboard*, November 19, 2024. www.billboard.com.

9. Quoted in "Dua Lipa on Leaving Bad Relationships."

FOR FURTHER RESEARCH

BOOKS

Tammy Gagne, *Refugee and Immigrant Rights*. BrightPoint Press, 2025.

Carolyn McHugh, *Mwah—Dua Lipa: The Illustrated Biography*. Sona Books, 2025.

Keng Xiong, *Olivia Rodrigo*. BrightPoint Press, 2026.

INTERNET SOURCES

"Dua Lipa: The 60 Minutes Interview," *YouTube*, uploaded by 60 Minutes, February 9, 2025. www.youtube.com.

Alex Marshall, "Can a Music Festival Make Kosovo Cool?" *New York Times*, August 17, 2018. www.nytimes.com.

"The Reasons We're Here: Oral Histories of Immigration at Portland Community College," *OpenOregon Educational Resources*, n.d. https://openoregon.pressbooks.pub.

WEBSITES

Sunny Hill Foundation
https://sunnyhillfoundation.org

Dua Lipa and her father established the Sunny Hill Foundation in 2016. Visit this website to see how they support art, culture, and sports in Kosovo.

Sunny Hill Music Festival
https://sunnyhillfestival.com

This annual music festival, held in Kosovo, is organized by the Sunny Hill Foundation. It brings musical artists together from all over the world.

The Trevor Project
www.thetrevorproject.org

The Trevor Project is a cause supported by Dua Lipa. It provides crisis support services for LGBTQ+ youth.

INDEX

IMAGE CREDITS

Cover: © Ryu Seung Il/Alamy
5: © agwilson/Shutterstock Images
7: © stock_photo_world/Shutterstock Images
9: © katatonia82/Shutterstock Images
10: © Featureflash Photo Agency/Shutterstock Images
13: © Opis Zagreb/Shutterstock Images
16: © Roman Voloshyn/Shutterstock Images
19: © MehmetO/Shutterstock Images
20: © madras91/Flickr
23: © Ben Houdijk/Shutterstock Images
25: © Christian Bertrand/Shutterstock Images
27: © Chrispictures/Shutterstock images
28: © xijian/iStockphoto
31: © Fred Duval/Shutterstock Images
32: © Featureflash Photo Agency/Shutterstock Images
37: © fotografiko eugen/Shutterstock Images
39: © Dfp Photographic/Shutterstock Images
40: © Benny Hawes/Shutterstock Images
44: © David M. Benett/Getty Images for the Elton John AIDS Foundation/Dave Benett Collection/Getty Images
47: © Red Line Editorial
49: © Armend Nimani/AFP/Getty Images
51: © Kathy Hutchins/Shutterstock Images
53: © Fred Duval/Shutterstock Images
55: © Armend Nimani/AFP/Getty Images
56: © Raphael Rivest/Shutterstock Images

ABOUT THE AUTHOR

Heather L. Bode is an elementary educator. She loves researching and writing nonfiction books for young people and adults. Other interests include traveling, baking, and hanging out with family. She lives in Minneapolis, Minnesota.